ADVENTURES IN COLONIAL AMERICA

BOSTON TEA PARTY

Rebellion in the Colonies

by James E. Knight

illustrated by David Wenzel

Troll

Library of Congress Cataloging-in-Publication Data

Knight, James E.
    Boston Tea Party.

    Summary: A Boston merchant describes the American
colonists' act of protest against British taxation and
the tea monopoly of the East India Company.
    1. Boston Tea Party, 1773—Juvenile literature.
[1. Boston Tea Party, 1773.   2. United States—History—
Revolution, 1775–1783—Causes] I. Wenzel, David,
1950–   ill. II. Title.
E215.7.K54   973.3'115   81-23077
ISBN 0-89375-734-9 (lib. bdg.)   AACR2
ISBN 0-8167-4802-0 (pbk.)

This edition published in 2001.

Printed in the United States of America.

10   9   8   7   6

BOSTON TEA PARTY

Rebellion in the Colonies

June 18, 1774

Mr. William Yancy
Committee of Correspondence
James Street, Charleston
Royal Province of South Carolina

Dear Mr. Yancy:

Samuel Adams paid me a visit last evening and asked me to write to you. He feels our work in the Committee of Correspondence is more important than ever. We in the several Colonies must keep each other informed. Only then can we stand truly united against British oppression.

To that end, Mr. Adams has urged me to inform you of the true facts, which have brought about our plight here. I refer to the destruction of the tea on the evening of December 16, 1773. This event some now call the "Tea Party" in Boston Harbor. So that you and the citizens of Charleston may know how it came about, I shall relate the details of the event.

I have been a merchant in this city for fifteen years, and I deal heavily in tea. Until the hated taxes of the Townshend Acts were thrust upon us, I did well enough and made a profit. Then, as you know, Britain repealed the Townshend Acts—but left the tax on tea.

That is when my business began to do poorly. People refused to buy English tea because of the tax upon it. Some bought tax-free black-market tea, which was smuggled in from Holland. Others stopped drinking tea altogether.

Large stocks of English tea began to rot in London warehouses. The East India Company asked Parliament for help, and the Tea Act of 1773 was passed.

The Act gave the East India a shameful monopoly on all tea trade with the American Colonies. It permitted the Company to price English tea—even with the tax on it—*lower* than our smuggled tea! By offering tea at this low price, the British felt certain they could sell their tea in great quantities.

We merchants were quick to realize one thing. If ships loaded with English tea reached our shores, we would soon be ruined. The East India Company had appointed

special Tea Agents to receive the low-priced tea here in America. These Tea Agents were not ordinary merchants like ourselves. Far from it. They were either friends or relatives of our Royal Governors and Judges. By flooding the market with their tea, the Tea Agents would reap quick profits—and colonial merchants would be driven out of business.

In November of 1773, three ships were on their way to Boston—loaded with chests of East India Company tea. Should all this tea be allowed to land, we would find our own tea trade at once undercut. True, some colonists would continue to boycott English tea. But others would certainly buy the inexpensive tea.

Fearing for our livelihood, we turned for help to the Sons of Liberty. These patriots were in great sympathy with us. They agreed that the tea must not be allowed ashore, and that the ships must be sent back to England. Messages were sent to the Tea Agents, demanding that they resign their positions. Of course, the Agents refused.

At that point, a group of young townspeople attacked one of the Agent's warehouses. They threw goods about and caused much mischief. This so frightened the Agents that they fled with their families to Castle Island, the British fortress that guards the entrance to Boston Harbor.

With each passing day, we grew more anxious. The hated tea ships were due to arrive at any time. More fiery meetings were held, both private and public. Sam Adams often took charge at these gatherings. He is our most outspoken leader against British oppression. He has made speeches, written pamphlets, and composed songs—all in the name of liberty. In fact, last year he stirred such an uproar against British troops being quartered in the city that two regiments were removed to Castle Island.

Some smile at the way he dresses, for his stockings are often rumpled and his waistcoat wrongly buttoned. But one soon forgets such things when his strong voice rings out over the crowd.

At one particularly fiery meeting last November, Mr. Adams stood up and said, "It is a shameful thing which Parliament does to us. A tax on tea is still a tax, is it not? Do we Americans have a voice in Parliament to protest against it? We do not. It is but another example of taxation without representation. And that, my fellow countrymen, is tyranny!"

A few days later, on November 28, the first of the tea ships arrived and dropped anchor near Castle Island. It was the *Dartmouth*, a small whaler built in Nantucket. We learned that the other two ships would be along in a few days and would tie up at Griffin's Wharf.

I believe you've heard of our Boston Selectmen, Mr. Yancy? They are the men chosen to run the town's business. Well, a few hours after the *Dartmouth* docked, the Selectmen called a public meeting at Faneuil Hall. But the crowd that appeared was so large that the meeting was moved to the Old South Church.

The angry townspeople kept crying, "No tea landed here! No tea! No tea!" After Sam Adams made a short speech, the Selectmen voted that a guard of volunteers should be formed. These guards would stand watch at Griffin's Wharf to make sure no tea was taken ashore.

Next, the Selectmen voted to demand that the Tea Agents ship the tea back to England. They sent a messenger out to Castle Island to persuade them to do this. But the Tea Agents replied that they had not yet received their instructions from the East India Company and were therefore not responsible for the tea. They said that they had no right to send the tea back to England—and warned that if anything happened to it, the people of Boston would be held responsible.

There was much shouting and protesting among the townspeople. Then one of the Selectmen got to his feet and made a daring proposal. "Rather than let the tea come ashore," he shouted over the crowd, "could we not throw it overboard?" The people responded with cries of, "Yes! Into the water! Into the water with the tea!"

But nothing was done that night. Or for the next few days. We watched in silence as the *Dartmouth* left Castle Island and docked at Griffin's Wharf. The second tea ship, the *Eleanor*, arrived the next day and tied up at the same dock. A few days later, the third tea ship, the *Beaver*, dropped anchor out in the harbor. We heard there was sickness aboard, and that the *Beaver* would come in to dock later.

On December 13, the *Beaver* tied up at Griffin's Wharf. There they were—all three ships at the same dock—waiting to be unloaded. Even though our volunteers were on guard, we knew the Tea Agents would soon take steps to claim their cargo. Tension was in the air. Everyone could feel it. We wondered what would happen now.

The next afternoon, the largest mass meeting ever held in Boston assembled in and around Old South Church. Sam Adams and others made rousing speeches against the Tea Act. Then the Selectmen sent messages to the ship owners demanding that the ships be sent back to England.

But the owners replied that they could not do this, since they would not be allowed out of the harbor without paying the duty on the tea they had carried in. If they tried, they said, British warships would surely sink them!

One of the owners, Mr. Francis Rotch, appeared before the meeting. Rotch, who owns the *Dartmouth*, was willing to remove his ship from Boston. He said he would go to the Customhouse and try to get permission to leave. Another meeting was called for the 16th, to find out how he had fared.

A light snow was falling that morning as the meeting was called to order. Tempers were hot—and they grew even hotter when the crowd learned that Mr. Rotch's request to remove the *Dartmouth* had been turned down. The Selectmen then demanded that Rotch go directly to the Royal Governor and ask for a pass to leave the harbor. The meeting was adjourned until late afternoon. This would give Rotch time to meet with the Governor and return to Boston.

While everyone was waiting for the Governor's reply,

the Sons of Liberty were holding a meeting. I was there, for I knew that my business would be ruined if the tea was ever unloaded. At the meeting, everybody agreed that if Governor Hutchinson would not allow the ships to leave Boston, the tea must be destroyed.

"But who will do the job?" someone shouted.

"A volunteer group," said one of the leaders—Mr. Ebenezer Stevens.

So a number of volunteers stepped forward—and I was among them.

For several minutes we talked among ourselves—planning how best we could board the ships and get at the chests of tea. Someone suggested we disguise ourselves—perhaps as Mohawk Indians. If we did this, no one would know who had destroyed the tea. We could protect our names and families from British anger—and keep the Redcoats from our doors.

"Of course," said Ebenezer, "we shall deceive no one into thinking we are real Indians. But what does that matter? It is concealing our identities that counts."

So it was settled. We agreed to meet at Ebenezer's house across from the Old South Church—should the Governor refuse Rotch's request. Ebenezer's brother and another man agreed to provide the disguises and to supply us with axes to break open the tea chests.

Dusk had fallen by the time Mr. Rotch returned. A large crowd had gathered in the Old South Church to hear what news he brought. I stood just inside the entrance. Beside me was Paul Revere, the silversmith and frequent messenger for our Committee of Correspondence. As we learned the bad news, I felt Paul's hand grip my arm. The Governor had refused Rotch permission to leave Boston with his ship.

Sam Adams quickly took charge of the meeting. There was silence as he rose to speak. We waited to hear his *exact* words—for if they were the right ones, they would be our signal to destroy the tea.

"This meeting," announced Sam Adams, "can do nothing more to save the country."

A number of men around me began whooping and yelling in the manner of an Indian war party. Paul and I rushed with the others across the square to Ebenezer Stevens's house.

Once inside, we quickly put on our disguises. I chose an old blanket to wrap around me and a woman's shawl for my head. Others dressed in cast-off dresses, hoods, blankets, and woolen caps. We smeared our faces with ashes, chimney soot, red clay, and axle grease. In a few minutes, we could hardly recognize each other. None of us wore feathers or other Indian headdress. I fear that was a fanciful touch added by an artist for the Boston newspaper.

So disguised, we "Indians" left Ebenezer's house and hurried through the narrow streets toward the docks. We were joined by other volunteers at certain points along the way. Reaching Griffin's Wharf, we met for a final conference in an old warehouse. Then we formed into groups. Paul and I and a few others chose Ebenezer Stevens as our leader.

19

The moon raced in and out of the clouds as we strained to see the three tea ships. A light dusting of snow glistened in their rigging. There were only skeleton crews aboard, for most of the sailors had gone ashore. We decided that it would not be hard to take possession of the vessels and throw the tea into the harbor. One sentry was placed at the head of the wharf, and another in the middle. They would give the alarm if Tories, or others friendly to the British, came to the wharf.

Ebenezer said ours would be one of the groups to board the *Dartmouth*. Clutching our axes and hatchets, we crept up the gangway and onto the deck of the darkened ship. A couple of white-faced sailors did nothing to stop us. Then, we suddenly saw the captain blocking our way.

"Sir," said Ebenezer in a stern voice, "order your men to open the hatchways and hand us the hoisting tackle and ropes. Do as you are told and no harm will come to you."

"What do you intend to do?" asked the captain, staring fearfully at our painted faces.

20

"It's the tea we want, and it's the tea we'll have. Now do as I have said. Then get below."

They obeyed instantly—and soon we were about the business of holding our "Tea Party." There was a strange quiet on the ship as we worked. It was broken only by the ripping open of the tea chests and by numerous splashes in the water. Printed on each chest were the words: "Produce of East India Co.—TEA." Our work went swiftly, and there were no interruptions. As the chests of tea were hoisted on deck, we split them open until we could see the tea leaves inside. Then we pitched them overboard.

Paul Revere and I, laboring side by side, smashed away at box after box. It was hard work. Each wooden chest was wrapped in a canvas cover. Cutting away the canvas with our hatchets soon dulled the blades. Sometimes it would take too long to crack open a chest, and we simply flung it into the harbor unopened. Once I looked over the side and noticed that the water was stained dark from the tea.

One complication delayed our work that night. No one had thought to check the tides. At high tide, the water around Griffin's Wharf is only about as deep as a man is tall. At low tide it is only knee-deep. On that particular evening, the tide was dead low as we started our work. The vessels themselves were resting on the muddy bottom. The water was so shallow around the *Dartmouth* that the tea we threw overboard rapidly heaped up like stacks of hay. But a few boys jumped into the water—cold as it was—and pushed the chests out into deeper water.

Later, the tide began flooding into the harbor. The wrecked chests floated in toward shore. Some had already piled up on the beach under the docks. Since some of the tea might still be dry, we feared looting. We shouted at Ebenezer and pointed to the chests on shore.

"Don't worry," Ebenezer called, taking a mighty swing with his axe. "The tides will carry them out to sea in a few hours. Get on with your work."

We did. We kept hacking away at the chests and heaving them overboard. Spilled tea leaves crunched under our feet. Pausing at times to catch my breath, I could see other men with painted faces on the *Eleanor* and the *Beaver* doing the same work.

Word of what we were doing on Griffin's Wharf must have spread quickly through Boston. People began gathering on the docks to watch us. Some spectators waved. Others cheered each time a chest of tea splashed into the harbor.

We worked steadily at our task until after nine o'clock. My right arm began to ache from swinging my hatchet, so I started chopping awkwardly with the left. Then, suddenly, Paul and I stared at each other—the hoisting machinery had stopped.

There was no more tea in the *Dartmouth*'s hold. The job had taken us almost three hours. Breathing heavily from our labor, Paul and I sat down on a hatch cover to rest. We saw our leaders talking and nodding their heads vigorously. Then Ebenezer called us.

"We've got what we came for—the tea," he said. "Now we must sweep the decks clean and line up for inspection —just as we do on Militia Day. And woe to any man who has stolen a single leaf of the tea!"

And so it was done. The decks were swept down—all the stray tea and wood fragments were thrown over the side. Then we formed two columns, and our leaders passed among us to be sure no tea had been taken.

"This night's work is finished," Ebenezer said at last. "Let us go home."

With that, we marched off the *Dartmouth*, two by two, in good order. We could see other groups of men leaving the *Eleanor* and the *Beaver*. Weary as we were, we were in good spirits. As we marched up Fort Hill, I remember someone on Griffin's Wharf striking up a tune on a fife. It was "Yankee Doodle."

By ten o'clock that night, everyone—spectators and "Indians" alike—was safe at home. Everyone, that is, except Paul Revere. Exhausted as he was, he galloped off at the hour of midnight to carry the news of our "Tea Party" throughout the Colonies.

When I got home, I sat down before the fireplace and pulled off my boots. A shower of tea leaves fell upon the hearth. A neighbor, who had been keeping my wife company during my absence, exclaimed, "Oh, do save it! It will make a nice brew!"

28

But my Martha would not hear of it. Snatching up her broom, she swept the tea into the blazing fire.

In an accounting later, we learned that three hundred forty-two chests of tea had been thrown into the harbor that night. Of course, we refused to pay for the tea. And now, all of Boston is feeling the sting of Britain's anger.

On May 30, Boston Harbor was closed to all shipping. Regiments of British soldiers began to pour into the city. They have made our lives miserable. From the window where I sit, I can see a company of Redcoats parading in front of the State House. Boston has become an armed camp, and we are under martial law. The British commander, General Gage, rules a city in which hundreds are out of work. Hardship has made us all bitter. Business is at a standstill.

The Sons of Liberty continue to turn out leaflets of a violent nature against the British, but Gage ignores them. He thinks Britain will starve us into submission and make us pay for the tea. But he is mistaken. We shall not starve. Supplies are smuggled into the city by night. New York sends us flour for bread. Connecticut sends us sheep. Even so, if this continues, I fear there must soon be war.

Now I must seal this letter, and give it to Paul Revere, who is waiting to take it and other letters to the ship at Marblehead. This is how our mail must go these days, for Boston is blockaded.

Let us know how matters stand with you in South Carolina. I believe that we in Boston may be watching the beginning of a Revolution.

Yours in Liberty, I am your obedient servant,

Benjamin Hatcher
Committee of Correspondence
Boston, Prov. of Mass.

Index